50 Australian Appetizer Recipes for Home

By: Kelly Johnson

Table of Contents

- Mini Beef Pies
- Vegemite and Cheese Scrolls
- Smoked Salmon Blinis
- Chicken Satay Skewers
- Prawn Cocktail
- Kangaroo Sliders
- Oysters Kilpatrick
- Grilled Haloumi with Lemon
- Crab Cakes with Aioli
- Zucchini and Corn Fritters
- Stuffed Mushrooms with Cream Cheese and Bacon
- Aussie Meatballs with Tomato Chutney
- Grilled Prawns with Garlic Butter
- Potato Skins with Sour Cream and Chives
- Pumpkin Soup Shots
- Crocodile Sausage Rolls
- Beetroot and Goat Cheese Crostini
- Aussie Meat Pies
- Chicken and Avocado Sushi Rolls
- Lamb Koftas with Tzatziki
- Crispy Calamari with Aioli
- Roasted Capsicum and Feta Bruschetta
- BBQ Pork Ribs
- Veggie Spring Rolls with Sweet Chili Sauce
- Smoked Trout Dip with Crackers
- Grilled Octopus Salad
- Spinach and Ricotta Triangles
- Garlic Prawn Pizza
- Tuna Tartare with Avocado
- Pork Belly Bites with Apple Sauce
- Aussie Damper Bread with Butter and Honey
- Barramundi Ceviche
- Chicken Wings with BBQ Sauce
- Cheese and Bacon Stuffed Jalapenos
- Pesto and Sundried Tomato Pinwheels

- Tempura Vegetables with Dipping Sauce
- Crumbed Whiting Fillets with Tartare Sauce
- Mini Sausage Rolls with Tomato Relish
- Antipasto Platter with Olives, Cheese, and Cold Cuts
- Beef Skewers with Chimichurri Sauce
- Mushroom and Blue Cheese Tartlets
- Seafood Paella Balls
- Corn Chips with Guacamole and Salsa
- Tandoori Chicken Wings
- Feta and Olive Stuffed Peppers
- Chicken Liver Pate on Toast Points
- Aussie BBQ Shrimp
- Veggie and Cheese Mini Quiches
- Stuffed Dates with Prosciutto and Goat Cheese
- Grilled Lamb Cutlets with Mint Sauce

Mini Beef Pies

Ingredients:

For the pastry:

- 2 sheets of frozen puff pastry, thawed
- Flour (for dusting)

For the beef filling:

- 300g ground beef
- 1 small onion, finely chopped
- 1 carrot, diced
- 1 celery stalk, diced
- 2 garlic cloves, minced
- 1 tablespoon tomato paste
- 1 teaspoon Worcestershire sauce
- 1/2 teaspoon dried thyme
- Salt and pepper to taste
- 1 tablespoon olive oil
- 1/2 cup beef stock
- 1 tablespoon all-purpose flour (optional, for thickening)

Instructions:

1. Preheat your oven to 200°C (400°F) and line a baking tray with parchment paper.
2. In a large skillet or frying pan, heat the olive oil over medium heat. Add the chopped onion, carrot, and celery, and cook until softened, about 5-7 minutes.
3. Add the minced garlic and ground beef to the skillet. Cook, breaking up the beef with a spoon, until browned and cooked through.
4. Stir in the tomato paste, Worcestershire sauce, dried thyme, salt, and pepper. Cook for another 2 minutes.
5. If using, sprinkle the flour over the beef mixture and stir well to combine. This will help thicken the filling.

6. Pour in the beef stock and simmer for 5-7 minutes, or until the sauce has thickened slightly. Remove from heat and let the filling cool slightly.
7. While the filling is cooling, roll out the thawed puff pastry sheets on a lightly floured surface. Using a round cutter or a glass, cut out circles from the pastry, large enough to line the cups of a muffin tin.
8. Line each cup of the muffin tin with a circle of pastry, pressing gently to fit.
9. Spoon the cooled beef filling into each pastry-lined cup, filling them almost to the top.
10. Cut out smaller circles from the remaining pastry and use them to cover the pies. Press the edges to seal, and if desired, use a fork to crimp the edges.
11. Using a sharp knife, make a small slit in the center of each pie to allow steam to escape.
12. Place the muffin tin in the preheated oven and bake for 20-25 minutes, or until the pastry is golden brown and crispy.
13. Remove the mini beef pies from the oven and let them cool slightly before serving.

Enjoy these delicious Mini Beef Pies as appetizers or snacks!

Vegemite and Cheese Scrolls

Ingredients:

- 2 sheets of frozen puff pastry, thawed
- 3 tablespoons Vegemite
- 1 cup grated cheese (cheddar or mozzarella)
- 1 egg, beaten (for egg wash)

Instructions:

1. Preheat your oven to 200°C (400°F) and line a baking tray with parchment paper.
2. On a lightly floured surface, place one sheet of thawed puff pastry. Roll it out slightly to flatten and even it out.
3. Spread a thin layer of Vegemite evenly over the surface of the puff pastry sheet, leaving a small border around the edges.
4. Sprinkle grated cheese evenly over the Vegemite layer.
5. Starting from one edge, tightly roll up the puff pastry sheet into a log.
6. Repeat the process with the second sheet of puff pastry.
7. Using a sharp knife, cut the rolled-up pastry logs into slices, about 1 inch thick.
8. Place the slices onto the prepared baking tray, spacing them slightly apart.
9. Brush the tops of the scrolls with beaten egg to give them a golden brown color when baked.
10. Bake in the preheated oven for 15-20 minutes, or until the scrolls are puffed and golden brown.
11. Remove from the oven and let the scrolls cool slightly before serving.

Enjoy these delicious Vegemite and Cheese Scrolls as a tasty snack or appetizer!

They're perfect for serving at parties or enjoying with a cup of tea or coffee.

Smoked Salmon Blinis

Ingredients:

For the blinis:

- 1 cup all-purpose flour
- 1 teaspoon baking powder
- 1/2 teaspoon salt
- 1 cup milk
- 1 large egg
- 2 tablespoons melted butter
- Vegetable oil or butter for cooking

For serving:

- Smoked salmon slices
- Cream cheese or sour cream
- Fresh dill, chopped
- Lemon wedges

Instructions:

1. In a mixing bowl, whisk together the flour, baking powder, and salt.
2. In a separate bowl, whisk together the milk, egg, and melted butter until well combined.
3. Pour the wet ingredients into the dry ingredients and whisk until smooth. Let the batter rest for about 10 minutes.
4. Heat a non-stick skillet or griddle over medium heat and lightly grease it with vegetable oil or butter.
5. Once the skillet is hot, spoon small dollops of batter onto the skillet to form mini pancakes (about 2-3 inches in diameter).
6. Cook the blinis for 1-2 minutes on each side, or until golden brown and cooked through. You may need to adjust the heat to prevent them from burning.

7. Remove the cooked blinis from the skillet and transfer them to a plate lined with paper towels to absorb any excess oil.
8. To serve, top each blini with a slice of smoked salmon and a dollop of cream cheese or sour cream.
9. Garnish with chopped fresh dill and serve with lemon wedges on the side for squeezing over the salmon.
10. Arrange the smoked salmon blinis on a platter and serve immediately as a delicious appetizer or party snack.

Enjoy these delightful Smoked Salmon Blinis as a flavorful and elegant addition to your next gathering or brunch!

Chicken Satay Skewers

Ingredients:

For the chicken marinade:

- 1 lb (450g) boneless, skinless chicken breasts or thighs, cut into thin strips
- 2 tablespoons soy sauce
- 2 tablespoons fish sauce
- 2 tablespoons brown sugar
- 2 cloves garlic, minced
- 1 teaspoon ground coriander
- 1 teaspoon ground cumin
- 1/2 teaspoon turmeric
- 1 tablespoon vegetable oil

For the peanut sauce:

- 1/2 cup creamy peanut butter
- 1/4 cup coconut milk
- 2 tablespoons soy sauce
- 2 tablespoons brown sugar
- 1 tablespoon lime juice
- 1 teaspoon grated ginger
- 1 clove garlic, minced
- Pinch of red pepper flakes (optional)
- Water (as needed to thin)

For serving:

- Bamboo skewers, soaked in water for 30 minutes
- Chopped peanuts (optional, for garnish)
- Chopped fresh cilantro (optional, for garnish)
- Lime wedges (optional, for serving)

Instructions:

1. In a bowl, combine the soy sauce, fish sauce, brown sugar, minced garlic, ground coriander, ground cumin, turmeric, and vegetable oil to make the marinade.
2. Add the chicken strips to the marinade and toss until evenly coated. Cover the bowl and refrigerate for at least 1 hour, or overnight for best results.
3. While the chicken is marinating, prepare the peanut sauce. In a small saucepan, combine the peanut butter, coconut milk, soy sauce, brown sugar, lime juice, grated ginger, minced garlic, and red pepper flakes (if using). Heat over low heat, stirring constantly, until the sauce is smooth and well combined. If the sauce is too thick, thin it out with water until desired consistency is reached. Remove from heat and set aside.
4. Preheat your grill or grill pan to medium-high heat.
5. Thread the marinated chicken strips onto the soaked bamboo skewers, dividing them evenly among the skewers.
6. Grill the chicken skewers for 3-4 minutes on each side, or until cooked through and slightly charred.
7. Transfer the grilled chicken satay skewers to a serving platter.
8. Drizzle the peanut sauce over the skewers or serve it on the side for dipping.
9. Garnish with chopped peanuts and cilantro, if desired, and serve with lime wedges on the side for squeezing.
10. Enjoy these delicious Chicken Satay Skewers as an appetizer or main dish, accompanied by steamed rice and your favorite vegetables!

These Chicken Satay Skewers are perfect for serving at parties or as a flavorful addition to your next barbecue.

Prawn Cocktail

Ingredients:

For the cocktail sauce:

- 1/2 cup mayonnaise
- 2 tablespoons ketchup
- 1 tablespoon horseradish sauce (adjust to taste)
- 1 teaspoon Worcestershire sauce
- 1 teaspoon lemon juice
- Salt and pepper to taste

For the prawn cocktail:

- 1 lb (450g) cooked and peeled prawns (shrimp), chilled
- Lettuce leaves, for serving
- Lemon wedges, for garnish
- Chopped fresh parsley, for garnish

Instructions:

1. In a small bowl, whisk together the mayonnaise, ketchup, horseradish sauce, Worcestershire sauce, lemon juice, salt, and pepper to make the cocktail sauce. Adjust the seasoning and horseradish sauce to taste. Cover and refrigerate until ready to use.
2. Arrange the lettuce leaves on individual serving plates or in a large serving bowl to create a bed for the prawn cocktail.
3. Place the chilled cooked prawns on top of the lettuce leaves.
4. Spoon the cocktail sauce generously over the prawns, coating them evenly.
5. Garnish the prawn cocktail with lemon wedges and chopped fresh parsley for a pop of color and freshness.
6. Serve the prawn cocktail immediately, accompanied by additional lemon wedges and crusty bread or breadsticks, if desired.

7. Enjoy this classic Prawn Cocktail as a refreshing and elegant appetizer, perfect for any occasion!

Feel free to customize the cocktail sauce according to your taste preferences by adjusting the amounts of ketchup, horseradish sauce, and Worcestershire sauce. You can also add a dash of hot sauce for extra heat if you like it spicy.

Kangaroo Sliders

Ingredients:

For the kangaroo patties:

- 1 lb (450g) ground kangaroo meat
- 1 small onion, finely chopped
- 2 cloves garlic, minced
- 1 tablespoon Worcestershire sauce
- 1 tablespoon Dijon mustard
- Salt and pepper to taste
- Olive oil for cooking

For assembling the sliders:

- Slider buns or mini burger buns
- Lettuce leaves
- Tomato slices
- Red onion slices
- Pickles (optional)
- Cheese slices (your choice)
- Mayonnaise, ketchup, or your favorite condiments

Instructions:

1. In a large mixing bowl, combine the ground kangaroo meat with the chopped onion, minced garlic, Worcestershire sauce, Dijon mustard, salt, and pepper. Mix well until all the ingredients are evenly incorporated.
2. Divide the kangaroo mixture into equal-sized portions and shape them into small patties, slightly larger than the size of your slider buns. Make an indentation in the center of each patty with your thumb to prevent them from puffing up during cooking.
3. Heat a drizzle of olive oil in a skillet or grill pan over medium-high heat. Once hot, add the kangaroo patties to the skillet, working in batches if necessary to avoid overcrowding. Cook for 3-4 minutes on each side, or until the patties are browned and cooked through to your liking.

4. While the kangaroo patties are cooking, lightly toast the slider buns on a separate skillet or grill pan until golden brown.
5. Assemble the sliders by placing a kangaroo patty on the bottom half of each slider bun. Top with lettuce leaves, tomato slices, red onion slices, pickles (if using), cheese slices, and your favorite condiments.
6. Place the top half of the slider buns over the fillings to complete the sliders.
7. Serve the Kangaroo Sliders immediately, either as appetizers or as a main dish, accompanied by your favorite side dishes.

Enjoy these unique and flavorful Kangaroo Sliders with family and friends!

Oysters Kilpatrick

Ingredients:

- 12 fresh oysters, shucked
- 6 slices of bacon, diced
- 2 tablespoons Worcestershire sauce
- 1 tablespoon tomato ketchup
- 1 tablespoon brown sugar
- Dash of hot sauce (optional)
- Lemon wedges, for serving
- Fresh parsley, chopped, for garnish

Instructions:

1. Preheat your grill to high heat.
2. Arrange the shucked oysters on a baking sheet or ovenproof dish filled with rock salt to stabilize them.
3. In a skillet over medium heat, cook the diced bacon until crispy and golden brown. Remove the bacon from the skillet and drain on paper towels to remove excess grease.
4. In a small bowl, mix together the Worcestershire sauce, tomato ketchup, brown sugar, and hot sauce (if using) to make the sauce.
5. Spoon a small amount of the sauce over each oyster.
6. Top each oyster with a few pieces of crispy bacon.
7. Place the oysters under the preheated grill and cook for 3-5 minutes, or until the sauce is bubbly and the edges of the oysters start to curl.
8. Remove the Oysters Kilpatrick from the grill and transfer them to a serving platter.
9. Garnish with chopped fresh parsley and serve immediately with lemon wedges on the side.

Enjoy these delicious Oysters Kilpatrick as an appetizer or starter for a special meal!

The combination of succulent oysters, smoky bacon, and tangy sauce is sure to impress your guests.

Grilled Haloumi with Lemon

Ingredients:

- 1 block of haloumi cheese, sliced into 1/4-inch thick slices
- 1-2 tablespoons olive oil
- 1 lemon, cut into wedges
- Freshly ground black pepper, to taste
- Fresh herbs for garnish (optional)

Instructions:

1. Preheat your grill or grill pan to medium-high heat.
2. Brush the haloumi slices lightly with olive oil on both sides.
3. Place the haloumi slices on the preheated grill and cook for 1-2 minutes on each side, or until grill marks form and the cheese is heated through. Haloumi cheese doesn't melt like other cheeses, so it will retain its shape but become soft and slightly golden when grilled.
4. While the haloumi is grilling, place the lemon wedges on the grill as well and cook for 1-2 minutes on each side, or until slightly charred and caramelized.
5. Once the haloumi slices are grilled to your liking, remove them from the grill and transfer them to a serving platter.
6. Squeeze the grilled lemon wedges over the haloumi slices to add a burst of fresh citrus flavor.
7. Season the grilled haloumi with freshly ground black pepper to taste.
8. Garnish with fresh herbs, such as parsley or mint, if desired.
9. Serve the Grilled Haloumi with Lemon immediately while hot.

Enjoy the irresistible combination of smoky grilled haloumi cheese and zesty grilled lemon for a delightful appetizer or side dish that's perfect for summer entertaining!

Crab Cakes with Aioli

Ingredients:

For the crab cakes:

- 1 lb (450g) lump crabmeat, drained
- 1/2 cup breadcrumbs (panko or regular)
- 1/4 cup mayonnaise
- 1 large egg, beaten
- 2 tablespoons chopped fresh parsley
- 1 tablespoon Dijon mustard
- 1 tablespoon Worcestershire sauce
- 1 teaspoon Old Bay seasoning (or to taste)
- Salt and pepper to taste
- 2 tablespoons olive oil (for frying)

For the aioli:

- 1/2 cup mayonnaise
- 1 garlic clove, minced
- 1 tablespoon lemon juice
- 1 teaspoon Dijon mustard
- Salt and pepper to taste

Instructions:

1. In a large mixing bowl, combine the lump crabmeat, breadcrumbs, mayonnaise, beaten egg, chopped parsley, Dijon mustard, Worcestershire sauce, Old Bay seasoning, salt, and pepper. Gently fold the ingredients together until evenly mixed, being careful not to break up the crabmeat too much.
2. Form the crab mixture into small patties, about 2 inches in diameter and 1/2 inch thick. Place the patties on a baking sheet lined with parchment paper and refrigerate for at least 30 minutes to firm up.

3. While the crab cakes are chilling, prepare the aioli. In a small bowl, combine the mayonnaise, minced garlic, lemon juice, Dijon mustard, salt, and pepper. Stir well to combine. Cover and refrigerate until ready to serve.
4. Heat the olive oil in a large skillet over medium heat. Once hot, add the crab cakes to the skillet in batches, being careful not to overcrowd the pan. Cook for 3-4 minutes on each side, or until golden brown and crispy.
5. Transfer the cooked crab cakes to a plate lined with paper towels to drain off any excess oil.
6. Serve the crab cakes hot, accompanied by the prepared aioli for dipping.
7. Garnish with additional chopped parsley or a squeeze of lemon juice if desired.
8. Enjoy these delicious Crab Cakes with Aioli as a tasty appetizer or light main course!

These crab cakes are bursting with flavor from the lump crabmeat and seasonings, while the aioli adds a creamy and zesty touch that perfectly complements the dish.

Zucchini and Corn Fritters

Ingredients:

- 2 medium zucchinis
- 1 cup fresh or frozen corn kernels
- 1/2 cup all-purpose flour
- 1/4 cup grated Parmesan cheese
- 2 cloves garlic, minced
- 2 green onions, finely chopped
- 2 large eggs, beaten
- Salt and pepper to taste
- Olive oil for frying
- Sour cream or Greek yogurt for serving (optional)
- Fresh herbs for garnish (optional)

Instructions:

1. Grate the zucchinis using a box grater or food processor. Place the grated zucchini in a clean kitchen towel and squeeze out excess moisture.
2. In a large mixing bowl, combine the grated zucchini, corn kernels, flour, grated Parmesan cheese, minced garlic, chopped green onions, beaten eggs, salt, and pepper. Stir until all ingredients are well combined and the mixture holds together.
3. Heat a thin layer of olive oil in a large skillet over medium heat.
4. Once the oil is hot, drop spoonfuls of the zucchini and corn mixture into the skillet, flattening them slightly with the back of the spoon to form fritters. Cook the fritters in batches, being careful not to overcrowd the pan.
5. Fry the fritters for 2-3 minutes on each side, or until golden brown and crispy. Use a spatula to flip them halfway through cooking.
6. Once cooked, transfer the fritters to a plate lined with paper towels to absorb any excess oil.
7. Repeat the process with the remaining zucchini and corn mixture until all the fritters are cooked.
8. Serve the zucchini and corn fritters hot, garnished with a dollop of sour cream or Greek yogurt and fresh herbs if desired.
9. Enjoy these delicious fritters as a tasty appetizer, snack, or light meal!

These zucchini and corn fritters are packed with flavor and have a lovely crispy texture on the outside, with tender zucchini and sweet corn on the inside. They're perfect for using up any excess zucchini you may have and are sure to be a hit with family and friends.

Stuffed Mushrooms with Cream Cheese and Bacon

Ingredients:

- 12 large mushrooms, cleaned with stems removed
- 6 slices of bacon, cooked and crumbled
- 4 oz (113g) cream cheese, softened
- 1/4 cup grated Parmesan cheese
- 2 cloves garlic, minced
- 2 green onions, finely chopped
- Salt and pepper to taste
- Olive oil or cooking spray

Instructions:

1. Preheat your oven to 375°F (190°C). Line a baking sheet with parchment paper or aluminum foil.
2. In a mixing bowl, combine the softened cream cheese, grated Parmesan cheese, minced garlic, chopped green onions, and cooked crumbled bacon. Mix until well combined. Season with salt and pepper to taste.
3. Using a spoon, fill each mushroom cap with the cream cheese and bacon mixture, pressing it down slightly to fill the cavity.
4. Place the stuffed mushrooms on the prepared baking sheet, spacing them slightly apart.
5. Drizzle or spray the mushrooms lightly with olive oil or cooking spray to help them brown in the oven.
6. Bake the stuffed mushrooms in the preheated oven for 20-25 minutes, or until the mushrooms are tender and the filling is golden brown and bubbly.
7. Remove the stuffed mushrooms from the oven and let them cool slightly before serving.
8. Serve the stuffed mushrooms warm as an appetizer or snack, garnished with additional chopped green onions or parsley if desired.

These stuffed mushrooms with cream cheese and bacon are sure to be a crowd-pleaser at any gathering. They're packed with flavor and have a satisfying combination of creamy and savory elements that make them irresistible!

Aussie Meatballs with Tomato Chutney

Ingredients:

For the meatballs:

- 1 lb (450g) ground beef or lamb
- 1/2 cup breadcrumbs
- 1/4 cup grated Parmesan cheese
- 1 egg
- 2 cloves garlic, minced
- 2 tablespoons chopped fresh parsley
- 1 teaspoon dried oregano
- Salt and pepper to taste
- Olive oil for cooking

For the tomato chutney:

- 1 tablespoon olive oil
- 1 small onion, finely chopped
- 2 cloves garlic, minced
- 1 (14 oz) can diced tomatoes
- 2 tablespoons brown sugar
- 2 tablespoons apple cider vinegar
- 1 teaspoon mustard seeds
- 1/2 teaspoon ground ginger
- 1/4 teaspoon ground cloves
- Salt and pepper to taste

Instructions:

1. Preheat your oven to 400°F (200°C). Line a baking sheet with parchment paper or aluminum foil.

2. In a large mixing bowl, combine the ground beef or lamb, breadcrumbs, grated Parmesan cheese, egg, minced garlic, chopped parsley, dried oregano, salt, and pepper. Mix until all ingredients are well combined.
3. Shape the meat mixture into small meatballs, about 1 inch in diameter, and place them on the prepared baking sheet.
4. Drizzle the meatballs lightly with olive oil and bake in the preheated oven for 15-20 minutes, or until cooked through and golden brown.
5. While the meatballs are baking, prepare the tomato chutney. Heat the olive oil in a saucepan over medium heat. Add the chopped onion and minced garlic and cook until softened and translucent.
6. Add the diced tomatoes, brown sugar, apple cider vinegar, mustard seeds, ground ginger, ground cloves, salt, and pepper to the saucepan. Stir well to combine.
7. Bring the mixture to a simmer and cook, stirring occasionally, for 15-20 minutes, or until the chutney has thickened and reduced slightly.
8. Once the meatballs are cooked, remove them from the oven and transfer them to a serving platter.
9. Spoon the tomato chutney over the meatballs, coating them evenly.
10. Serve the Aussie meatballs with tomato chutney hot, garnished with additional chopped parsley if desired.

These Aussie meatballs with tomato chutney are delicious served as an appetizer, snack, or main course. The combination of savory meatballs with tangy and slightly sweet tomato chutney is sure to be a hit with family and friends!

Grilled Prawns with Garlic Butter

Ingredients:

- 1 lb (450g) large prawns, peeled and deveined, tails intact
- 4 tablespoons unsalted butter, melted
- 4 cloves garlic, minced
- 1 tablespoon fresh lemon juice
- 1 tablespoon chopped fresh parsley
- Salt and pepper to taste
- Lemon wedges, for serving
- Additional chopped parsley, for garnish (optional)

Instructions:

1. Preheat your grill to medium-high heat.
2. In a small saucepan or microwave-safe bowl, melt the unsalted butter over low heat or in the microwave.
3. Add the minced garlic, fresh lemon juice, chopped parsley, salt, and pepper to the melted butter. Stir well to combine.
4. Thread the peeled and deveined prawns onto skewers, dividing them evenly among the skewers.
5. Brush the prawns generously with the garlic butter mixture, coating them evenly on all sides.
6. Place the prawn skewers on the preheated grill and cook for 2-3 minutes on each side, or until the prawns are pink and opaque, and slightly charred.
7. While the prawns are grilling, brush them with the remaining garlic butter mixture occasionally to keep them moist and flavorful.
8. Once cooked, remove the prawn skewers from the grill and transfer them to a serving platter.
9. Garnish the grilled prawns with additional chopped parsley if desired and serve immediately with lemon wedges on the side.
10. Enjoy these succulent Grilled Prawns with Garlic Butter as a delicious appetizer or main course!

These grilled prawns are bursting with flavor from the garlic butter marinade, and they're perfect for serving at your next outdoor gathering or barbecue. The combination of juicy prawns, fragrant garlic, and zesty lemon is simply irresistible!

Potato Skins with Sour Cream and Chives

Ingredients:

- 4 large russet potatoes
- Olive oil
- Salt and pepper to taste
- 1 cup sour cream
- 2 tablespoons chopped fresh chives
- Optional toppings: shredded cheese, cooked bacon bits, chopped green onions

Instructions:

1. Preheat your oven to 400°F (200°C). Line a baking sheet with parchment paper or aluminum foil for easy cleanup.
2. Scrub the potatoes clean and pat them dry with a paper towel. Prick each potato several times with a fork to allow steam to escape during baking.
3. Rub each potato with olive oil and sprinkle with salt and pepper.
4. Place the potatoes directly on the oven rack or on a baking sheet and bake for 45-60 minutes, or until the potatoes are tender when pierced with a fork.
5. Once the potatoes are cooked, remove them from the oven and let them cool slightly until they are safe to handle.
6. Slice each potato in half lengthwise, and use a spoon to scoop out the flesh, leaving about 1/4 inch of potato attached to the skin. Save the scooped-out potato flesh for another use (such as mashed potatoes).
7. Increase the oven temperature to 450°F (230°C).
8. Place the potato skins back on the baking sheet, cut side up. Brush the inside of each skin with a little more olive oil and sprinkle with additional salt and pepper if desired.
9. Bake the potato skins in the preheated oven for 10-15 minutes, or until they are crispy and golden brown.
10. While the potato skins are baking, prepare the sour cream topping. In a small bowl, mix together the sour cream and chopped fresh chives.
11. Once the potato skins are crispy and golden brown, remove them from the oven and let them cool slightly.

12. Spoon a dollop of the sour cream mixture onto each potato skin, and sprinkle with any optional toppings you like, such as shredded cheese, cooked bacon bits, or chopped green onions.
13. Serve the potato skins with sour cream and chives immediately as a delicious appetizer or snack.

These potato skins with sour cream and chives are sure to be a hit at your next gathering or game day party! They're crispy, creamy, and packed with flavor, making them a tasty and satisfying treat for any occasion.

Pumpkin Soup Shots

Ingredients:

- 2 cups pumpkin puree (homemade or canned)
- 1 onion, chopped
- 2 cloves garlic, minced
- 2 cups vegetable broth or chicken broth
- 1 cup coconut milk or heavy cream
- 2 tablespoons olive oil
- 1 teaspoon ground cumin
- 1/2 teaspoon ground cinnamon
- 1/4 teaspoon ground nutmeg
- Salt and pepper to taste
- Optional garnishes: toasted pumpkin seeds, drizzle of coconut milk, chopped fresh herbs

Instructions:

1. In a large pot, heat the olive oil over medium heat. Add the chopped onion and minced garlic, and sauté until softened and fragrant, about 5 minutes.
2. Add the pumpkin puree, vegetable broth or chicken broth, ground cumin, ground cinnamon, and ground nutmeg to the pot. Stir well to combine.
3. Bring the soup to a simmer, then reduce the heat to low and let it simmer gently for about 15-20 minutes to allow the flavors to meld together.
4. Once the soup has simmered, remove it from the heat and let it cool slightly.
5. Using an immersion blender or countertop blender, carefully blend the soup until smooth and creamy.
6. Return the blended soup to the pot, and stir in the coconut milk or heavy cream. Season with salt and pepper to taste.
7. Place the pot back on the stove over low heat, and gently warm the soup through, being careful not to let it boil.
8. Once the soup is heated through, remove it from the heat and ladle it into small shot glasses or espresso cups.
9. Garnish each pumpkin soup shot with toasted pumpkin seeds, a drizzle of coconut milk, and chopped fresh herbs if desired.

10. Serve the pumpkin soup shots immediately as a flavorful and festive appetizer or starter.

These pumpkin soup shots are perfect for serving at autumn gatherings, Thanksgiving dinners, or holiday parties. They're rich, creamy, and full of warming spices, making them a comforting and satisfying treat for your guests to enjoy!

Crocodile Sausage Rolls

Ingredients:

- 1 lb (450g) crocodile meat, ground (you can also use a mix of crocodile and pork or chicken)
- 1 package (about 375g) puff pastry, thawed if frozen
- 1 small onion, finely chopped
- 2 cloves garlic, minced
- 1/4 cup breadcrumbs
- 1 tablespoon Worcestershire sauce
- 1 teaspoon dried mixed herbs (such as thyme, oregano, and parsley)
- Salt and pepper to taste
- 1 egg, beaten (for egg wash)
- Sesame seeds or poppy seeds (optional, for sprinkling)

Instructions:

1. Preheat your oven to 400°F (200°C). Line a baking sheet with parchment paper or silicone baking mat.
2. In a large mixing bowl, combine the ground crocodile meat, finely chopped onion, minced garlic, breadcrumbs, Worcestershire sauce, dried mixed herbs, salt, and pepper. Mix until all ingredients are well combined.
3. Roll out the puff pastry on a lightly floured surface into a large rectangle, about 1/4 inch thick.
4. Cut the pastry lengthwise into two equal strips.
5. Divide the crocodile meat mixture into two portions and shape each portion into a long sausage shape that runs along the length of each pastry strip.
6. Brush one edge of each pastry strip with beaten egg.
7. Roll the pastry over the crocodile meat mixture, enclosing it completely and sealing the edges with the beaten egg-brushed edge. Press lightly to seal.
8. Cut each long sausage roll into smaller pieces, about 2 inches long, and place them seam-side down on the prepared baking sheet.
9. Brush the tops of the sausage rolls with beaten egg and sprinkle with sesame seeds or poppy seeds if desired.
10. Bake in the preheated oven for 20-25 minutes, or until the pastry is golden brown and crispy and the filling is cooked through.

11. Remove from the oven and let the crocodile sausage rolls cool slightly before serving.
12. Serve the crocodile sausage rolls warm as a delicious appetizer or snack, accompanied by your favorite dipping sauce.

These crocodile sausage rolls are sure to impress with their unique flavor and flaky pastry. They're perfect for serving at parties, gatherings, or as a special treat for adventurous eaters!

Beetroot and Goat Cheese Crostini

Ingredients:

- 1 large beetroot, cooked and peeled
- 4 oz (113g) goat cheese, softened
- 1 French baguette, thinly sliced
- 2 tablespoons olive oil
- 1 clove garlic, peeled and halved
- Salt and pepper to taste
- Fresh thyme leaves for garnish (optional)
- Balsamic glaze for drizzling (optional)

Instructions:

1. Preheat your oven to 375°F (190°C).
2. Slice the cooked and peeled beetroot into thin rounds.
3. Place the baguette slices on a baking sheet and brush both sides lightly with olive oil. Bake in the preheated oven for 8-10 minutes, or until the bread is crispy and lightly golden brown. Remove from the oven and let cool slightly.
4. Rub one side of each toasted baguette slice with the cut side of the garlic clove to infuse them with garlic flavor.
5. Spread a layer of softened goat cheese onto each toasted baguette slice.
6. Top each goat cheese-covered baguette slice with a round of cooked beetroot.
7. Season the beetroot and goat cheese crostini with salt and pepper to taste.
8. Garnish the crostini with fresh thyme leaves if desired, and drizzle with balsamic glaze for an extra touch of flavor.
9. Arrange the beetroot and goat cheese crostini on a serving platter and serve immediately as a delicious appetizer or snack.

These beetroot and goat cheese crostini are perfect for entertaining guests or enjoying as a light and flavorful snack. They're visually stunning, packed with flavor, and easy to make, making them a great choice for any occasion!

Aussie Meat Pies

Ingredients:

For the pastry:

- 2 1/2 cups all-purpose flour
- 1 teaspoon salt
- 1 cup unsalted butter, cold and cut into small cubes
- 6-8 tablespoons ice water

For the filling:

- 1 lb (450g) ground beef
- 1 onion, finely chopped
- 2 cloves garlic, minced
- 1 carrot, finely diced
- 1 celery stalk, finely diced
- 1 tablespoon tomato paste
- 1 cup beef broth
- 1 tablespoon Worcestershire sauce
- 1 teaspoon dried thyme
- Salt and pepper to taste
- 2 tablespoons all-purpose flour (optional, for thickening)

Instructions:

1. To make the pastry, combine the flour and salt in a large mixing bowl. Add the cold cubed butter and use a pastry cutter or your fingertips to work the butter into the flour until the mixture resembles coarse crumbs.
2. Gradually add the ice water, one tablespoon at a time, mixing with a fork until the dough just comes together. Be careful not to overwork the dough. You may not need to use all of the water.
3. Shape the dough into a ball, wrap it in plastic wrap, and refrigerate for at least 30 minutes to chill.

4. While the dough is chilling, prepare the filling. In a large skillet, cook the ground beef over medium heat until browned and cooked through. Drain any excess fat from the skillet.
5. Add the chopped onion, minced garlic, diced carrot, and diced celery to the skillet with the cooked ground beef. Cook, stirring occasionally, until the vegetables are softened.
6. Stir in the tomato paste, beef broth, Worcestershire sauce, dried thyme, salt, and pepper. If you prefer a thicker filling, you can stir in 2 tablespoons of flour at this point to help thicken the mixture. Cook for a few more minutes until the sauce has thickened slightly. Remove from heat and let cool.
7. Preheat your oven to 375°F (190°C). Grease a 12-cup muffin tin.
8. On a lightly floured surface, roll out the chilled pastry dough to about 1/8 inch thickness. Use a round cutter or a drinking glass to cut out circles of dough slightly larger than the size of the muffin tin cups.
9. Press each circle of dough into the muffin tin cups, allowing the edges to hang over the sides.
10. Fill each pastry-lined cup with the cooled meat filling.
11. Fold the overhanging edges of the pastry dough over the filling to cover it completely, pressing the edges to seal.
12. Use a sharp knife to make a small slit or vent in the top of each pie to allow steam to escape during baking.
13. Place the muffin tin in the preheated oven and bake for 25-30 minutes, or until the pastry is golden brown and cooked through.
14. Remove the Aussie meat pies from the oven and let them cool slightly before serving.
15. Serve the Aussie meat pies warm as a delicious and hearty meal, perfect for lunch or dinner.

These Aussie meat pies are sure to be a hit with their flaky pastry crust and flavorful meat filling. Enjoy them on their own or with your favorite condiments, such as ketchup or HP sauce.

Chicken and Avocado Sushi Rolls

Ingredients:

- 2 cups sushi rice
- 2 1/2 cups water
- 1/4 cup rice vinegar
- 2 tablespoons sugar
- 1 teaspoon salt
- 2 boneless, skinless chicken breasts
- Salt and pepper to taste
- 1 ripe avocado, thinly sliced
- 4 sheets nori seaweed
- Soy sauce, pickled ginger, and wasabi for serving

Instructions:

1. Rinse the sushi rice in a fine mesh sieve under cold running water until the water runs clear. Drain well.
2. In a rice cooker or saucepan, combine the rinsed sushi rice and water. Cook the rice according to the manufacturer's instructions or bring to a boil, then reduce the heat to low, cover, and simmer for 18-20 minutes, or until the rice is tender and the water is absorbed.
3. In a small saucepan, combine the rice vinegar, sugar, and salt. Heat over low heat, stirring until the sugar and salt are dissolved. Remove from heat and let cool.
4. Once the rice is cooked, transfer it to a large bowl and gently fold in the seasoned rice vinegar mixture until well combined. Let the rice cool to room temperature.
5. While the rice is cooling, season the chicken breasts with salt and pepper. Heat a grill pan or skillet over medium-high heat and cook the chicken for 6-8 minutes per side, or until cooked through and no longer pink in the center. Remove from heat and let cool slightly before slicing into thin strips.
6. Place a bamboo sushi rolling mat on a flat surface and cover it with a sheet of plastic wrap. Place a sheet of nori seaweed, shiny side down, on the plastic wrap.
7. Wet your hands with water to prevent sticking, and spread a thin layer of sushi rice evenly over the nori seaweed, leaving a 1-inch border along the top edge.
8. Arrange slices of avocado and cooked chicken strips horizontally across the center of the rice-covered nori seaweed.

9. Using the bamboo sushi rolling mat, carefully roll up the sushi, starting from the bottom edge closest to you and rolling away from you, using gentle pressure to shape the roll. Roll until the seam is on the bottom and the sushi roll is tightly wrapped.
10. Using a sharp knife, moistened with water to prevent sticking, slice the sushi roll into bite-sized pieces.
11. Repeat the process with the remaining nori seaweed sheets, rice, avocado, and chicken.
12. Serve the chicken and avocado sushi rolls with soy sauce, pickled ginger, and wasabi on the side for dipping.

Enjoy these delicious homemade chicken and avocado sushi rolls as a healthy and flavorful meal or snack!

Lamb Koftas with Tzatziki

Ingredients:

For the lamb koftas:

- 1 lb (450g) ground lamb
- 1 small onion, finely chopped
- 2 cloves garlic, minced
- 2 tablespoons fresh parsley, chopped
- 1 teaspoon ground cumin
- 1 teaspoon ground coriander
- 1/2 teaspoon ground paprika
- 1/4 teaspoon ground cinnamon
- Salt and pepper to taste
- Olive oil, for grilling

For the tzatziki:

- 1 cup Greek yogurt
- 1/2 cucumber, grated and squeezed to remove excess moisture
- 1 clove garlic, minced
- 1 tablespoon lemon juice
- 1 tablespoon chopped fresh dill (or mint)
- Salt and pepper to taste

Instructions:

1. In a large mixing bowl, combine the ground lamb, finely chopped onion, minced garlic, chopped parsley, ground cumin, ground coriander, ground paprika, ground cinnamon, salt, and pepper. Mix well until all ingredients are evenly combined.
2. Divide the lamb mixture into equal portions and shape each portion into a sausage-like shape, forming them around metal skewers if desired.
3. Preheat a grill or grill pan to medium-high heat. Brush the grill grates lightly with olive oil to prevent sticking.
4. Place the lamb koftas on the preheated grill and cook for 4-5 minutes per side, or until they are cooked through and have grill marks on all sides.

5. While the lamb koftas are cooking, prepare the tzatziki sauce. In a medium bowl, combine the Greek yogurt, grated cucumber, minced garlic, lemon juice, chopped fresh dill (or mint), salt, and pepper. Stir until well combined.
6. Taste the tzatziki sauce and adjust seasoning if necessary. Refrigerate until ready to serve.
7. Once the lamb koftas are cooked, remove them from the grill and let them rest for a few minutes.
8. Serve the lamb koftas hot with the tzatziki sauce on the side for dipping.

Enjoy these delicious lamb koftas with tzatziki as a main dish or appetizer. They're packed with Mediterranean flavors and are sure to be a hit at your next gathering or barbecue!

Crispy Calamari with Aioli

Ingredients:

For the crispy calamari:

- 1 lb (450g) squid (calamari), cleaned and tubes sliced into rings
- 1 cup all-purpose flour
- 1 teaspoon salt
- 1/2 teaspoon black pepper
- 1/2 teaspoon paprika
- Vegetable oil, for frying

For the aioli:

- 1/2 cup mayonnaise
- 1 clove garlic, minced
- 1 tablespoon lemon juice
- 1 teaspoon Dijon mustard
- Salt and pepper to taste

Instructions:

1. Start by preparing the aioli. In a small bowl, combine the mayonnaise, minced garlic, lemon juice, Dijon mustard, salt, and pepper. Mix well until smooth and creamy. Taste and adjust seasoning if needed. Cover the bowl and refrigerate the aioli until ready to serve.
2. In a shallow dish, combine the all-purpose flour, salt, black pepper, and paprika. Mix well to combine.
3. Heat vegetable oil in a large skillet or deep fryer to 350°F (175°C).
4. Working in batches, dredge the calamari rings in the seasoned flour mixture, shaking off any excess flour.
5. Carefully lower the coated calamari rings into the hot oil and fry for 2-3 minutes, or until golden brown and crispy. Be careful not to overcrowd the skillet or fryer, as this will lower the oil temperature and result in soggy calamari.

6. Using a slotted spoon or tongs, transfer the fried calamari rings to a plate lined with paper towels to drain any excess oil.
7. Repeat the dredging and frying process with the remaining calamari rings until all are cooked.
8. Serve the crispy calamari hot, accompanied by the aioli dipping sauce on the side.
9. Garnish the calamari with lemon wedges and chopped parsley if desired.

Enjoy these crispy calamari with aioli as a delicious appetizer or snack. The crispy coating combined with the tender calamari and creamy aioli dipping sauce is sure to be a hit with family and friends!

Roasted Capsicum and Feta Bruschetta

Ingredients:

- 2 large red or yellow bell peppers (capsicums)
- 1 tablespoon olive oil
- Salt and pepper to taste
- 1 French baguette, sliced into 1/2-inch thick slices
- 1 clove garlic, peeled and halved
- 4 oz (113g) feta cheese, crumbled
- Fresh basil leaves, chopped, for garnish (optional)
- Balsamic glaze, for drizzling (optional)

Instructions:

1. Preheat your oven's broiler to high. Line a baking sheet with aluminum foil.
2. Cut the bell peppers in half lengthwise and remove the seeds and membranes. Place the pepper halves, cut side down, on the prepared baking sheet.
3. Drizzle the olive oil over the pepper halves and season with salt and pepper.
4. Place the baking sheet under the broiler and roast the peppers for 10-15 minutes, or until the skins are charred and blistered.
5. Remove the peppers from the oven and immediately transfer them to a heatproof bowl. Cover the bowl tightly with plastic wrap and let the peppers steam for about 10 minutes. This will make it easier to peel off the skins.
6. Once the peppers have cooled slightly, peel off the charred skins and discard them. Slice the roasted peppers into thin strips.
7. Preheat a grill pan or skillet over medium heat. Place the baguette slices on the grill pan and toast them for 1-2 minutes on each side, or until lightly golden brown and crisp. Alternatively, you can toast the bread in a toaster or under the broiler.
8. Rub each toasted baguette slice with the cut side of the garlic clove to infuse them with garlic flavor.
9. Top each toasted baguette slice with a few strips of roasted capsicum and a sprinkle of crumbled feta cheese.
10. Garnish the bruschetta with chopped fresh basil leaves if desired, and drizzle with balsamic glaze for an extra touch of flavor.

11. Serve the roasted capsicum and feta bruschetta immediately as a delicious appetizer or snack.

Enjoy the vibrant flavors and textures of this roasted capsicum and feta bruschetta as a tasty starter for your next gathering or as a light and satisfying snack!

BBQ Pork Ribs

Ingredients:

For the pork ribs:

- 2 racks of pork ribs (baby back ribs or St. Louis-style ribs)
- BBQ rub or seasoning of your choice
- BBQ sauce (homemade or store-bought)

For the BBQ rub:

- 2 tablespoons brown sugar
- 1 tablespoon smoked paprika
- 1 tablespoon garlic powder
- 1 tablespoon onion powder
- 1 tablespoon chili powder
- 1 teaspoon ground cumin
- 1 teaspoon salt
- 1/2 teaspoon black pepper
- 1/2 teaspoon cayenne pepper (optional, for heat)

Instructions:

1. Preheat your grill to medium-low heat (about 275°F to 300°F or 135°C to 150°C) for indirect grilling.
2. In a small bowl, mix together all the ingredients for the BBQ rub until well combined.
3. Pat the pork ribs dry with paper towels. Remove the thin membrane from the back of the ribs if present, as it can become tough during cooking and prevent the seasoning from penetrating the meat. Use a knife to loosen one end of the membrane, then grip it with a paper towel and peel it off.
4. Season both sides of the ribs generously with the BBQ rub, pressing the seasoning into the meat to adhere.

5. Place the seasoned ribs on the grill over indirect heat, bone side down. Close the lid and cook for 2 to 2 1/2 hours, or until the ribs are tender and the meat has pulled back from the ends of the bones.
6. During the last 30 minutes of cooking, baste the ribs with your favorite BBQ sauce, using a brush to apply a thick and even coating.
7. Continue cooking the ribs for another 30 minutes, allowing the BBQ sauce to caramelize and form a sticky glaze on the surface of the ribs.
8. Once the ribs are done, remove them from the grill and let them rest for a few minutes before slicing and serving.
9. Serve the BBQ pork ribs hot, accompanied by extra BBQ sauce on the side for dipping, and your favorite sides like coleslaw, cornbread, or baked beans.

These BBQ pork ribs are sure to be a hit with their tender, juicy meat and smoky, flavorful crust. Enjoy them at your next cookout or family gathering!

Veggie Spring Rolls with Sweet Chili Sauce

Ingredients:

For the spring rolls:

- 8-10 spring roll rice paper wrappers
- 2 cups mixed vegetables, thinly sliced or julienned (such as carrots, bell peppers, cucumber, lettuce, avocado, and bean sprouts)
- 1/2 cup fresh herbs (such as cilantro, mint, and Thai basil), chopped
- Cooked vermicelli noodles (optional)

For the sweet chili sauce:

- 1/4 cup sweet chili sauce
- 1 tablespoon soy sauce
- 1 tablespoon rice vinegar
- 1 teaspoon sesame oil
- 1 teaspoon grated ginger
- 1 clove garlic, minced
- Red pepper flakes or sriracha sauce (optional, for heat)

Instructions:

1. Prepare the sweet chili sauce by whisking together the sweet chili sauce, soy sauce, rice vinegar, sesame oil, grated ginger, minced garlic, and red pepper flakes or sriracha sauce (if using) in a small bowl. Set aside.
2. Prepare all the vegetables and herbs, slicing or julienning them into thin strips. If using vermicelli noodles, cook them according to the package instructions, then drain and rinse under cold water.
3. Fill a large shallow dish or pie plate with warm water. Dip one rice paper wrapper into the warm water for about 10-15 seconds, or until it becomes soft and pliable.
4. Carefully transfer the softened rice paper wrapper to a clean, damp kitchen towel or cutting board.

5. Arrange a small handful of the sliced vegetables, herbs, and vermicelli noodles (if using) in the center of the rice paper wrapper, leaving about an inch of space on each side.
6. Fold the bottom edge of the rice paper wrapper over the filling, then fold in the sides, and roll tightly to enclose the filling completely.
7. Repeat the process with the remaining rice paper wrappers and filling ingredients.
8. Serve the veggie spring rolls immediately with the sweet chili sauce for dipping, or cover them with a damp kitchen towel and refrigerate until ready to serve.
9. If refrigerated, bring the spring rolls to room temperature before serving.
10. Garnish the spring rolls with additional fresh herbs and serve as a light and refreshing appetizer or snack.

These veggie spring rolls with sweet chili sauce are versatile and customizable, making them a great option for parties, potlucks, or as a healthy snack. Enjoy the crisp, fresh flavors and the sweet and tangy kick of the dipping sauce!

Smoked Trout Dip with Crackers

Ingredients:

- 8 oz (225g) smoked trout, skin removed and flaked
- 8 oz (225g) cream cheese, softened
- 1/4 cup sour cream
- 2 tablespoons mayonnaise
- 1 tablespoon lemon juice
- 1 teaspoon Dijon mustard
- 2 green onions, thinly sliced (optional)
- 1 tablespoon chopped fresh dill (optional)
- Salt and pepper to taste
- Crackers or bread slices for serving

Instructions:

1. In a mixing bowl, combine the softened cream cheese, sour cream, mayonnaise, lemon juice, and Dijon mustard. Mix until smooth and well combined.
2. Add the flaked smoked trout to the cream cheese mixture. If desired, reserve a small amount of trout for garnish.
3. Add the thinly sliced green onions and chopped fresh dill to the bowl. Season with salt and pepper to taste.
4. Gently fold all the ingredients together until the smoked trout is evenly distributed throughout the dip.
5. Transfer the smoked trout dip to a serving bowl and garnish with any reserved smoked trout, green onions, or dill.
6. Serve the smoked trout dip immediately with crackers or bread slices for dipping.
7. Alternatively, cover the bowl with plastic wrap and refrigerate the dip for at least 1 hour to allow the flavors to meld together before serving.
8. Enjoy the smoked trout dip with crackers as a delicious appetizer or snack!

This creamy and flavorful smoked trout dip is sure to be a hit with its rich, smoky flavor and smooth texture. Serve it at your next gathering and watch it disappear!

Grilled Octopus Salad

Ingredients:

For the octopus:

- 1 large octopus (about 2-3 lbs / 900g - 1.4kg), cleaned and prepared
- 1/4 cup olive oil
- 2 cloves garlic, minced
- 2 tablespoons lemon juice
- Salt and pepper to taste

For the salad:

- Mixed salad greens (such as arugula, spinach, or mesclun)
- Cherry tomatoes, halved
- Cucumber, sliced
- Red onion, thinly sliced
- Kalamata olives
- Feta cheese, crumbled
- Lemon wedges for serving

For the dressing:

- 1/4 cup extra virgin olive oil
- 2 tablespoons lemon juice
- 1 teaspoon Dijon mustard
- 1 clove garlic, minced
- Salt and pepper to taste

Instructions:

1. Preheat your grill to medium-high heat.

2. In a large bowl, whisk together the olive oil, minced garlic, lemon juice, salt, and pepper to create a marinade for the octopus.
3. Add the cleaned octopus to the marinade, making sure it is well coated. Let it marinate for at least 30 minutes, or up to 2 hours in the refrigerator.
4. Once marinated, remove the octopus from the marinade and grill it over medium-high heat for 3-4 minutes per side, or until it is charred and cooked through. The tentacles should curl up and become firm when cooked.
5. Remove the grilled octopus from the grill and let it rest for a few minutes before slicing it into bite-sized pieces.
6. In a small bowl, whisk together the ingredients for the dressing: extra virgin olive oil, lemon juice, Dijon mustard, minced garlic, salt, and pepper. Adjust seasoning to taste.
7. Assemble the salad by arranging the mixed salad greens, cherry tomatoes, cucumber slices, red onion slices, Kalamata olives, and crumbled feta cheese on a serving platter.
8. Top the salad with the sliced grilled octopus.
9. Drizzle the dressing over the salad or serve it on the side.
10. Serve the grilled octopus salad immediately, garnished with lemon wedges for squeezing over the salad.

Enjoy this vibrant and flavorful grilled octopus salad as a delicious and satisfying meal!

Spinach and Ricotta Triangles

Ingredients:

For the filling:

- 1 tablespoon olive oil
- 1 small onion, finely chopped
- 2 cloves garlic, minced
- 6 cups fresh spinach leaves, chopped
- 1 cup ricotta cheese
- 1/2 cup grated Parmesan cheese
- 1/4 cup chopped fresh parsley
- 1/4 teaspoon ground nutmeg
- Salt and pepper to taste

For assembling:

- 1 package (about 20 sheets) phyllo pastry, thawed if frozen
- 1/2 cup unsalted butter, melted

Instructions:

1. Preheat your oven to 375°F (190°C). Line a baking sheet with parchment paper or lightly grease it.
2. Heat the olive oil in a large skillet over medium heat. Add the chopped onion and minced garlic and cook until softened and fragrant, about 2-3 minutes.
3. Add the chopped spinach to the skillet and cook until wilted, stirring occasionally, about 3-4 minutes. Remove from heat and let the spinach mixture cool slightly.
4. In a large mixing bowl, combine the cooked spinach mixture, ricotta cheese, grated Parmesan cheese, chopped parsley, ground nutmeg, salt, and pepper. Mix well until all ingredients are evenly combined. Taste and adjust seasoning if needed.
5. Place one sheet of phyllo pastry on a clean work surface. Brush the entire sheet with melted butter. Place another sheet of phyllo pastry on top and brush with

melted butter. Repeat this process until you have a stack of 5 sheets of phyllo pastry.
6. Cut the stacked phyllo pastry into long strips, about 3 inches wide.
7. Place a spoonful of the spinach and ricotta mixture at one end of each strip of phyllo pastry.
8. Fold one corner of the phyllo pastry over the filling to form a triangle. Continue folding the triangle over itself until you reach the end of the strip. Brush the outside of the triangle with melted butter to seal it.
9. Repeat this process with the remaining phyllo pastry strips and filling mixture.
10. Place the assembled spinach and ricotta triangles on the prepared baking sheet.
11. Bake in the preheated oven for 15-20 minutes, or until the triangles are golden brown and crispy.
12. Remove from the oven and let the triangles cool slightly before serving.

Enjoy these delicious spinach and ricotta triangles as a tasty appetizer or snack! They're perfect for parties, gatherings, or as a light meal paired with a salad.

Garlic Prawn Pizza

Ingredients:

For the pizza dough:

- 1 pound (450g) pizza dough, store-bought or homemade
- Cornmeal or flour, for dusting

For the garlic prawns:

- 1 pound (450g) large prawns, peeled and deveined
- 4 cloves garlic, minced
- 2 tablespoons olive oil
- Salt and pepper to taste
- Crushed red pepper flakes (optional, for heat)

For the pizza toppings:

- 1 cup shredded mozzarella cheese
- 1/2 cup grated Parmesan cheese
- 2 tablespoons chopped fresh parsley or basil
- Lemon wedges for serving

Instructions:

1. Preheat your oven to the highest temperature setting (usually around 475°F to 500°F or 245°C to 260°C). If you have a pizza stone, place it in the oven while preheating.
2. In a skillet, heat the olive oil over medium heat. Add the minced garlic and cook for 1-2 minutes, or until fragrant.
3. Add the prawns to the skillet and season with salt, pepper, and crushed red pepper flakes (if using). Cook the prawns for 2-3 minutes on each side, or until they are pink and opaque. Remove from heat and set aside.
4. On a lightly floured surface, roll out the pizza dough into a circle or rectangle, depending on your preference and the shape of your baking sheet or pizza stone.

5. Sprinkle cornmeal or flour on a baking sheet or pizza peel to prevent the pizza from sticking.
6. Transfer the rolled-out pizza dough to the prepared baking sheet or pizza peel.
7. Spread the shredded mozzarella cheese evenly over the pizza dough, leaving a border around the edges for the crust.
8. Arrange the cooked garlic prawns evenly over the cheese.
9. Sprinkle the grated Parmesan cheese over the prawns.
10. Transfer the pizza to the preheated oven and bake for 10-12 minutes, or until the crust is golden brown and the cheese is melted and bubbly.
11. Remove the pizza from the oven and sprinkle chopped fresh parsley or basil over the top.
12. Serve the garlic prawn pizza hot, with lemon wedges on the side for squeezing over the pizza before eating.

Enjoy this delicious garlic prawn pizza as a flavorful and satisfying meal!

Tuna Tartare with Avocado

Ingredients:

- 8 oz (225g) sushi-grade tuna, diced into small cubes
- 1 ripe avocado, diced into small cubes
- 1 tablespoon soy sauce
- 1 teaspoon sesame oil
- 1 teaspoon rice vinegar
- 1 teaspoon fresh lime juice
- 1 teaspoon honey or maple syrup (optional)
- 1 tablespoon finely chopped shallots or red onion
- 1 tablespoon chopped fresh cilantro or parsley
- 1 teaspoon black or white sesame seeds
- Salt and pepper to taste
- Thinly sliced green onions or chives for garnish (optional)
- Toasted sesame seeds for garnish (optional)
- Tortilla chips or crispy wonton wrappers for serving

Instructions:

1. In a mixing bowl, combine the diced tuna, diced avocado, soy sauce, sesame oil, rice vinegar, lime juice, honey or maple syrup (if using), chopped shallots or red onion, chopped cilantro or parsley, and sesame seeds. Gently toss until all ingredients are evenly coated.
2. Taste the tuna tartare and season with salt and pepper as needed.
3. Cover the bowl with plastic wrap and refrigerate the tuna tartare for at least 30 minutes to allow the flavors to meld together.
4. When ready to serve, divide the tuna tartare mixture among serving plates or bowls.
5. Garnish the tuna tartare with thinly sliced green onions or chives and toasted sesame seeds, if desired.
6. Serve the tuna tartare with tortilla chips or crispy wonton wrappers on the side for scooping and dipping.
7. Enjoy the tuna tartare with avocado as a light and flavorful appetizer!

This tuna tartare with avocado is perfect for entertaining guests or enjoying as a special treat at home. The combination of fresh tuna, creamy avocado, and tangy seasonings creates a delicious dish that's sure to impress!

Pork Belly Bites with Apple Sauce

Ingredients:

For the pork belly:

- 1 lb (450g) pork belly, skin removed and cut into bite-sized cubes
- 1 tablespoon olive oil
- Salt and pepper to taste

For the apple sauce:

- 2 large apples, peeled, cored, and diced
- 1 tablespoon unsalted butter
- 2 tablespoons brown sugar
- 1/2 teaspoon ground cinnamon
- Pinch of nutmeg
- Pinch of salt

Instructions:

1. Preheat your oven to 375°F (190°C). Line a baking sheet with parchment paper or aluminum foil for easy cleanup.
2. Pat the pork belly cubes dry with paper towels to remove excess moisture.
3. In a large bowl, toss the pork belly cubes with olive oil, salt, and pepper until evenly coated.
4. Arrange the seasoned pork belly cubes in a single layer on the prepared baking sheet.
5. Roast the pork belly in the preheated oven for 30-40 minutes, or until golden brown and crispy on the outside and tender on the inside. Flip the pork belly cubes halfway through the cooking time for even browning.
6. While the pork belly is roasting, prepare the apple sauce. In a saucepan, melt the butter over medium heat.
7. Add the diced apples to the saucepan and cook, stirring occasionally, until they begin to soften, about 5-7 minutes.

8. Stir in the brown sugar, ground cinnamon, nutmeg, and salt. Continue cooking the apples until they are tender and caramelized, about 5-7 minutes more.
9. Remove the saucepan from the heat and use a potato masher or fork to mash the cooked apples into a chunky sauce. If you prefer a smoother sauce, you can blend it with an immersion blender or food processor.
10. Once the pork belly is done, remove it from the oven and let it cool slightly.
11. Serve the crispy pork belly bites with the homemade apple sauce on the side for dipping.
12. Enjoy these delicious pork belly bites with apple sauce as a crowd-pleasing appetizer or snack!

These pork belly bites with apple sauce are sure to be a hit at your next gathering with their irresistible combination of crispy pork and sweet, tangy apple flavors.

Aussie Damper Bread with Butter and Honey

Ingredients:

- 3 cups self-raising flour
- 1 teaspoon salt
- 1 cup water
- Butter, for serving
- Honey, for serving

Instructions:

1. Preheat your oven to 400°F (200°C). Line a baking sheet with parchment paper or lightly grease it.
2. In a large mixing bowl, sift the self-raising flour and salt together.
3. Gradually add the water to the flour mixture, stirring with a wooden spoon or your hands, until a dough forms. The dough should come together easily and not be too sticky.
4. Turn the dough out onto a lightly floured surface and knead it gently for a few minutes until smooth.
5. Shape the dough into a round loaf and place it on the prepared baking sheet.
6. Use a sharp knife to score a cross on the top of the loaf, about 1/2 inch deep. This helps the bread to cook evenly.
7. Bake the damper bread in the preheated oven for 30-40 minutes, or until it is golden brown on top and sounds hollow when tapped on the bottom.
8. Remove the damper bread from the oven and transfer it to a wire rack to cool slightly.
9. Once cooled, slice the damper bread into thick slices and serve warm with butter and honey.
10. Enjoy this Aussie damper bread with butter and honey as a tasty snack or accompaniment to soups, stews, or barbecued meats.

This simple and rustic Aussie damper bread is perfect for enjoying with friends and family, especially when served warm with lashings of butter and honey!

Barramundi Ceviche

Ingredients:

- 1 lb (450g) fresh barramundi fillets, skin removed and diced into small cubes
- 4-5 limes, juiced
- 2 lemons, juiced
- 1 orange, juiced
- 1 small red onion, finely chopped
- 1 red bell pepper, finely diced
- 1 jalapeño pepper, seeded and finely chopped
- 1/4 cup chopped fresh cilantro
- 1/4 cup chopped fresh parsley
- 1/4 cup chopped fresh mint
- 2 tablespoons extra virgin olive oil
- Salt and pepper to taste
- Optional garnishes: avocado slices, cherry tomatoes, cucumber slices, radish slices, tortilla chips or crackers

Instructions:

1. In a non-reactive bowl, combine the diced barramundi fillets with the lime juice, lemon juice, and orange juice. Make sure the fish is completely submerged in the citrus juice. Cover the bowl with plastic wrap and refrigerate for at least 30 minutes to marinate. The acid in the citrus juice will "cook" the fish, turning it opaque and firm.
2. While the fish is marinating, prepare the vegetables and herbs. Finely chop the red onion, red bell pepper, jalapeño pepper, cilantro, parsley, and mint. You can adjust the amount of jalapeño pepper to your desired level of heat.
3. After the fish has marinated, drain off most of the citrus juice, leaving just enough to coat the fish. The fish should be opaque and firm to the touch.
4. Add the chopped red onion, red bell pepper, jalapeño pepper, cilantro, parsley, mint, and extra virgin olive oil to the bowl with the marinated fish. Season with salt and pepper to taste.
5. Gently toss all the ingredients together until evenly combined.
6. Cover the bowl again with plastic wrap and refrigerate the barramundi ceviche for another 15-30 minutes to allow the flavors to meld together.

7. Before serving, taste the ceviche and adjust the seasoning if needed.
8. Serve the barramundi ceviche chilled, garnished with avocado slices, cherry tomatoes, cucumber slices, radish slices, and tortilla chips or crackers on the side.
9. Enjoy the fresh and vibrant flavors of this barramundi ceviche as a light and refreshing appetizer or main course!

Note: Make sure to use fresh, high-quality barramundi fillets for the best results in this ceviche recipe.

Chicken Wings with BBQ Sauce

Ingredients:

For the chicken wings:

- 2 lbs (about 1 kg) chicken wings, split into drumettes and wingettes
- 2 tablespoons olive oil
- Salt and pepper to taste
- Optional: garlic powder, onion powder, paprika, or other seasonings of your choice

For the BBQ sauce:

- 1 cup ketchup
- 1/4 cup apple cider vinegar
- 1/4 cup brown sugar
- 2 tablespoons honey
- 2 tablespoons Worcestershire sauce
- 1 tablespoon Dijon mustard
- 1 teaspoon smoked paprika
- 1/2 teaspoon garlic powder
- Salt and pepper to taste

Instructions:

1. Preheat your oven to 400°F (200°C). Line a baking sheet with aluminum foil and lightly grease it with cooking spray or olive oil.
2. In a large bowl, toss the chicken wings with olive oil, salt, pepper, and any optional seasonings you like. Make sure the wings are evenly coated.
3. Arrange the seasoned chicken wings in a single layer on the prepared baking sheet.
4. Bake the chicken wings in the preheated oven for 40-45 minutes, or until they are golden brown and crispy, flipping them halfway through cooking for even browning.
5. While the chicken wings are baking, prepare the BBQ sauce. In a saucepan, combine the ketchup, apple cider vinegar, brown sugar, honey, Worcestershire

sauce, Dijon mustard, smoked paprika, garlic powder, salt, and pepper. Stir well to combine.
6. Bring the BBQ sauce to a simmer over medium heat, then reduce the heat to low and let it simmer gently for 10-15 minutes, stirring occasionally, until the sauce has thickened slightly.
7. Once the chicken wings are cooked through and crispy, remove them from the oven and transfer them to a large mixing bowl.
8. Pour the BBQ sauce over the cooked chicken wings and toss them until they are evenly coated in the sauce.
9. Return the sauced chicken wings to the baking sheet and bake for an additional 5-10 minutes, or until the sauce is caramelized and sticky.
10. Remove the chicken wings from the oven and let them cool slightly before serving.
11. Serve the BBQ chicken wings hot, garnished with chopped fresh parsley or green onions if desired.
12. Enjoy these delicious BBQ chicken wings as a tasty appetizer or main dish! Serve them with celery sticks, carrot sticks, and ranch or blue cheese dressing on the side for dipping.

Cheese and Bacon Stuffed Jalapenos

Ingredients:

- 12 large jalapeno peppers
- 8 oz (225g) cream cheese, softened
- 1 cup shredded cheddar cheese
- 1/2 cup cooked and crumbled bacon
- 2 green onions, finely chopped
- 1 teaspoon garlic powder
- 1/2 teaspoon paprika
- Salt and pepper to taste
- Optional: toothpicks for securing the jalapeno halves

Instructions:

1. Preheat your oven to 375°F (190°C). Line a baking sheet with aluminum foil or parchment paper for easy cleanup.
2. Cut the jalapeno peppers in half lengthwise and remove the seeds and membranes. Use a spoon to scrape out any remaining seeds and create a hollow cavity in each jalapeno half.
3. In a mixing bowl, combine the softened cream cheese, shredded cheddar cheese, crumbled bacon, chopped green onions, garlic powder, paprika, salt, and pepper. Mix until all ingredients are well combined.
4. Spoon the cheese and bacon mixture into each jalapeno half, filling them evenly and pressing the mixture down slightly.
5. If desired, secure the jalapeno halves with toothpicks to prevent them from tipping over during baking.
6. Place the stuffed jalapenos on the prepared baking sheet, spacing them apart slightly.
7. Bake in the preheated oven for 20-25 minutes, or until the jalapenos are softened and the cheese is melted and bubbly.
8. Remove the stuffed jalapenos from the oven and let them cool slightly before serving.
9. Serve the cheese and bacon stuffed jalapenos hot, garnished with additional chopped green onions or fresh herbs if desired.

10. Enjoy these delicious appetizers as a crowd-pleasing snack or party food! Be sure to warn guests that they're spicy and to handle them with care due to the heat of the jalapenos.

Pesto and Sundried Tomato Pinwheels

Ingredients:

- 1 sheet puff pastry, thawed
- 1/4 cup prepared pesto
- 1/4 cup sundried tomatoes, drained and chopped
- 1/4 cup grated Parmesan cheese
- 1 tablespoon chopped fresh basil (optional)
- Egg wash (1 egg beaten with 1 tablespoon water), for brushing

Instructions:

1. Preheat your oven to 400°F (200°C). Line a baking sheet with parchment paper for easy cleanup.
2. On a lightly floured surface, roll out the thawed puff pastry sheet into a rectangle, about 12x10 inches in size.
3. Spread the prepared pesto evenly over the surface of the puff pastry sheet, leaving a small border around the edges.
4. Sprinkle the chopped sundried tomatoes, grated Parmesan cheese, and chopped fresh basil (if using) evenly over the pesto.
5. Starting from one long edge, tightly roll up the puff pastry sheet into a log, like a jelly roll. Seal the edge by brushing it lightly with egg wash.
6. Using a sharp knife, slice the puff pastry log into 1/2-inch thick rounds. You should get about 10-12 pinwheels, depending on the size of your puff pastry sheet.
7. Place the pinwheels cut side down on the prepared baking sheet, spacing them apart slightly.
8. Brush the tops of the pinwheels with egg wash for a golden finish.
9. Bake in the preheated oven for 15-20 minutes, or until the pinwheels are puffed up and golden brown.
10. Remove the pinwheels from the oven and let them cool slightly before serving.
11. Serve the pesto and sundried tomato pinwheels warm or at room temperature as a delicious appetizer or snack.

These pinwheels are best served fresh but can also be stored in an airtight container in the refrigerator for up to 2 days. Simply reheat them in the oven before serving, if desired. Enjoy!

Tempura Vegetables with Dipping Sauce

Ingredients:

For the tempura batter:

- 1 cup all-purpose flour
- 1/2 cup cornstarch
- 1 teaspoon baking powder
- 1 teaspoon salt
- 1 1/4 cups ice-cold water

For the vegetables:

- Assorted vegetables, such as bell peppers, zucchini, carrots, broccoli, sweet potatoes, or mushrooms, cut into bite-sized pieces

For the dipping sauce:

- 1/4 cup soy sauce
- 2 tablespoons rice vinegar
- 1 tablespoon mirin (sweet rice wine) or honey
- 1 teaspoon grated ginger
- 1 teaspoon minced garlic
- 1 tablespoon chopped green onions or cilantro (optional)
- Pinch of red pepper flakes (optional)

Instructions:

1. Prepare the dipping sauce by combining the soy sauce, rice vinegar, mirin or honey, grated ginger, minced garlic, chopped green onions or cilantro (if using), and red pepper flakes (if using) in a small bowl. Stir well to combine and set aside.

2. In a large mixing bowl, whisk together the all-purpose flour, cornstarch, baking powder, and salt.
3. Gradually add the ice-cold water to the flour mixture, whisking constantly, until you have a smooth batter. The batter should have a thin consistency, similar to pancake batter. Be careful not to overmix.
4. Heat vegetable oil in a deep fryer or large pot to 350°F (175°C).
5. Dip the assorted vegetables into the tempura batter, making sure they are evenly coated.
6. Carefully place the battered vegetables into the hot oil, a few pieces at a time, making sure not to overcrowd the pot. Fry the vegetables in batches for 2-3 minutes, or until they are golden brown and crispy.
7. Use a slotted spoon or tongs to remove the fried vegetables from the oil and transfer them to a plate lined with paper towels to drain excess oil.
8. Serve the tempura vegetables hot with the dipping sauce on the side for dipping.
9. Enjoy the crispy and delicious tempura vegetables as a tasty appetizer or snack!

Feel free to customize the dipping sauce to your taste by adjusting the ingredients. You can also experiment with different vegetables to create your own unique tempura combination. Enjoy!

Crumbed Whiting Fillets with Tartare Sauce

Ingredients:

For the crumbed whiting fillets:

- 4 whiting fillets, skin removed
- 1 cup breadcrumbs (you can use store-bought or homemade)
- 1/2 cup all-purpose flour
- 2 eggs, beaten
- Salt and pepper to taste
- Vegetable oil, for frying
- Lemon wedges, for serving

For the tartare sauce:

- 1/2 cup mayonnaise
- 2 tablespoons chopped pickles or gherkins
- 1 tablespoon capers, chopped
- 1 tablespoon chopped fresh parsley
- 1 tablespoon lemon juice
- 1 teaspoon Dijon mustard
- Salt and pepper to taste

Instructions:

1. Prepare the tartare sauce by combining the mayonnaise, chopped pickles or gherkins, chopped capers, chopped fresh parsley, lemon juice, Dijon mustard, salt, and pepper in a small bowl. Stir well to combine, then taste and adjust the seasoning if needed. Cover and refrigerate until ready to serve.
2. Season the whiting fillets with salt and pepper on both sides.
3. Set up a breading station with three shallow dishes: one with flour, one with beaten eggs, and one with breadcrumbs.
4. Dredge each whiting fillet in the flour, shaking off any excess.
5. Dip the floured fillets into the beaten eggs, allowing any excess to drip off.

6. Coat the fillets in breadcrumbs, pressing gently to adhere. Repeat the process for each fillet, ensuring they are evenly coated.
7. Heat vegetable oil in a large skillet over medium heat. Add enough oil to cover the bottom of the skillet.
8. Once the oil is hot, carefully add the breaded whiting fillets to the skillet. Fry for 3-4 minutes on each side, or until golden brown and crispy. Be careful not to overcrowd the skillet; you may need to fry the fillets in batches.
9. Once cooked, transfer the fried whiting fillets to a plate lined with paper towels to drain any excess oil.
10. Serve the crumbed whiting fillets hot with tartare sauce on the side for dipping, and lemon wedges for squeezing over the fish.
11. Enjoy this delicious seafood dish as a main course or appetizer, paired with your favorite sides!

Feel free to customize the tartare sauce by adding ingredients like chopped onions, garlic, or herbs to suit your taste preferences.

Mini Sausage Rolls with Tomato Relish

Ingredients:

For the mini sausage rolls:

- 1 sheet puff pastry, thawed
- 8-10 small pork sausages (or chicken sausages), casings removed
- 1 egg, beaten (for egg wash)

For the tomato relish:

- 1 cup chopped tomatoes
- 1/4 cup chopped onions
- 2 cloves garlic, minced
- 2 tablespoons brown sugar
- 2 tablespoons apple cider vinegar
- 1/2 teaspoon smoked paprika
- Salt and pepper to taste

Instructions:

1. Preheat your oven to 400°F (200°C). Line a baking sheet with parchment paper for easy cleanup.
2. To make the tomato relish, combine the chopped tomatoes, chopped onions, minced garlic, brown sugar, apple cider vinegar, smoked paprika, salt, and pepper in a small saucepan. Stir well to combine.
3. Bring the mixture to a simmer over medium heat, then reduce the heat to low and let it simmer gently for 15-20 minutes, stirring occasionally, until the tomatoes break down and the relish thickens slightly. Remove from heat and let it cool.
4. While the tomato relish is cooking, prepare the mini sausage rolls. Roll out the thawed puff pastry sheet on a lightly floured surface into a rectangle, about 12x10 inches in size.
5. Divide the sausage meat into 8-10 portions, depending on the size of your sausages.

6. Place a portion of sausage meat along one long edge of the puff pastry rectangle. Roll up the pastry tightly, enclosing the sausage meat. Repeat with the remaining sausage meat and pastry.
7. Cut each rolled-up sausage roll into 3-4 smaller pieces, depending on the desired size of your mini sausage rolls.
8. Place the mini sausage rolls seam side down on the prepared baking sheet.
9. Brush the tops of the sausage rolls with beaten egg for a golden finish.
10. Bake in the preheated oven for 20-25 minutes, or until the pastry is golden brown and the sausage meat is cooked through.
11. Remove the mini sausage rolls from the oven and let them cool slightly before serving.
12. Serve the warm mini sausage rolls with the homemade tomato relish on the side for dipping.
13. Enjoy these delicious mini sausage rolls with tomato relish as a tasty appetizer or snack!

Feel free to customize the sausage rolls by adding herbs, spices, or grated cheese to the sausage meat mixture for extra flavor.

Antipasto Platter with Olives, Cheese, and Cold Cuts

Ingredients:

For the antipasto platter:

- Assorted olives (such as Kalamata, green, or mixed)
- Assorted cheeses (such as mozzarella, provolone, Parmesan, or goat cheese)
- Assorted cold cuts (such as salami, prosciutto, ham, or mortadella)
- Marinated artichoke hearts
- Roasted red peppers
- Cherry tomatoes
- Grilled or marinated vegetables (such as zucchini, eggplant, or bell peppers)
- Breadsticks or sliced baguette
- Crackers or bread slices
- Fresh herbs for garnish (such as basil or parsley)

Instructions:

1. Start by arranging a large platter or wooden board to serve as the base for your antipasto spread.
2. Place small bowls or ramekins on the platter to hold the olives and any dips or spreads you may be serving, such as hummus or tapenade.
3. Arrange the assorted cheeses on the platter, either sliced or in chunks. Mix and match different types of cheese for variety and flavor.
4. Arrange the assorted cold cuts on the platter, either folded or rolled up. Arrange them in an attractive pattern around the cheeses.
5. Fill in the empty spaces on the platter with marinated artichoke hearts, roasted red peppers, cherry tomatoes, and grilled or marinated vegetables. You can also add other antipasto items such as pickles, sun-dried tomatoes, or marinated mushrooms.
6. Place breadsticks or sliced baguette on the platter for guests to enjoy with the cheeses and cold cuts.
7. Add crackers or bread slices to the platter for additional variety and texture.
8. Garnish the platter with fresh herbs, such as basil or parsley, for a pop of color and flavor.
9. Serve the antipasto platter at room temperature and encourage guests to help themselves to their favorite items.

10. Enjoy the delicious flavors and variety of your homemade antipasto platter with olives, cheese, and cold cuts!

Feel free to customize your antipasto platter with other items such as nuts, dried fruits, or fresh fruit slices, depending on your preferences and what's available. The key is to create a beautiful and delicious spread that will delight your guests and satisfy their appetites.

Beef Skewers with Chimichurri Sauce

Ingredients:

For the beef skewers:

- 1 1/2 lbs (680g) beef sirloin or flank steak, cut into 1-inch cubes
- Wooden or metal skewers, soaked in water if using wooden ones
- Salt and pepper to taste
- Olive oil for brushing

For the chimichurri sauce:

- 1 cup fresh parsley, chopped
- 1/4 cup fresh cilantro, chopped
- 3 cloves garlic, minced
- 1/4 cup red wine vinegar
- 1/2 cup extra virgin olive oil
- 1 tablespoon fresh oregano leaves (or 1 teaspoon dried oregano)
- 1/2 teaspoon red pepper flakes (optional)
- Salt and pepper to taste

Instructions:

1. If using wooden skewers, soak them in water for at least 30 minutes to prevent them from burning during grilling.
2. In a medium bowl, season the beef cubes with salt, pepper, and a drizzle of olive oil. Toss to coat evenly.
3. Thread the seasoned beef cubes onto the skewers, leaving a little space between each piece.
4. Preheat your grill or grill pan to medium-high heat.
5. While the grill is heating up, prepare the chimichurri sauce. In a food processor or blender, combine the chopped parsley, chopped cilantro, minced garlic, red wine vinegar, extra virgin olive oil, fresh oregano leaves, and red pepper flakes (if using). Pulse until the herbs are finely chopped and the ingredients are well

combined. Season with salt and pepper to taste. Transfer the chimichurri sauce to a serving bowl and set aside.
6. Once the grill is hot, brush the beef skewers lightly with olive oil to prevent sticking.
7. Grill the beef skewers for 3-4 minutes per side, or until they are cooked to your desired level of doneness. The internal temperature of the beef should reach at least 145°F (63°C) for medium-rare.
8. Remove the beef skewers from the grill and let them rest for a few minutes before serving.
9. Serve the grilled beef skewers hot, accompanied by the chimichurri sauce for dipping or drizzling over the top.
10. Enjoy these delicious beef skewers with chimichurri sauce as a main course or appetizer!

These beef skewers with chimichurri sauce are sure to be a hit at your next barbecue or dinner party. The flavorful marinade and zesty sauce complement the juicy beef perfectly, creating a dish that's bursting with flavor.

Mushroom and Blue Cheese Tartlets

Ingredients:

For the tartlet shells:

- 1 sheet puff pastry, thawed
- All-purpose flour, for dusting

For the mushroom and blue cheese filling:

- 2 tablespoons butter
- 1 tablespoon olive oil
- 1 lb (450g) mushrooms, thinly sliced (such as cremini or button mushrooms)
- 2 cloves garlic, minced
- 1/4 cup chopped fresh parsley
- Salt and pepper to taste
- 4 oz (115g) blue cheese, crumbled (such as Roquefort or Gorgonzola)

Instructions:

1. Preheat your oven to 400°F (200°C). Lightly grease a mini muffin tin or tartlet pan with cooking spray or butter.
2. Roll out the thawed puff pastry sheet on a lightly floured surface. Using a round cookie cutter or a glass, cut out circles of dough slightly larger than the muffin tin or tartlet molds.
3. Press the puff pastry circles into the prepared muffin tin or tartlet molds, gently pressing the dough up the sides to create small tartlet shells. Prick the bottoms of the tartlet shells with a fork to prevent them from puffing up too much during baking.
4. Bake the tartlet shells in the preheated oven for 10-12 minutes, or until they are lightly golden brown and puffed up. Remove from the oven and let them cool slightly.

5. While the tartlet shells are baking, prepare the mushroom and blue cheese filling. In a large skillet, heat the butter and olive oil over medium heat until the butter is melted.
6. Add the sliced mushrooms to the skillet and cook, stirring occasionally, until they are golden brown and tender, about 5-7 minutes.
7. Add the minced garlic to the skillet and cook for an additional 1-2 minutes, or until fragrant.
8. Stir in the chopped fresh parsley and season the mushroom mixture with salt and pepper to taste. Remove the skillet from the heat and let the mixture cool slightly.
9. Once the tartlet shells have cooled, spoon a small amount of the mushroom mixture into each shell, filling them about halfway.
10. Crumble the blue cheese over the top of each tartlet, dividing it evenly among them.
11. Return the filled tartlet shells to the oven and bake for an additional 5-7 minutes, or until the cheese is melted and bubbly.
12. Remove the mushroom and blue cheese tartlets from the oven and let them cool slightly before serving.
13. Serve the tartlets warm or at room temperature as a delicious appetizer or snack.

These mushroom and blue cheese tartlets are sure to impress your guests with their rich and savory flavors. Enjoy!

Seafood Paella Balls

Ingredients:

For the paella rice:

- 1 cup paella rice (such as Bomba or Arborio rice)
- 2 cups chicken or seafood broth
- Pinch of saffron threads (optional)
- 1 tablespoon olive oil
- 1 onion, finely chopped
- 2 cloves garlic, minced
- 1 red bell pepper, diced
- 1 tomato, diced
- 1 teaspoon smoked paprika
- 1/2 teaspoon turmeric
- Salt and pepper to taste
- 1/2 cup frozen peas, thawed
- 1/4 cup chopped fresh parsley

For the seafood filling:

- 8 oz (225g) mixed seafood (such as shrimp, squid, and mussels), cooked and chopped
- 1/4 cup chopped fresh parsley
- Salt and pepper to taste

For breading and frying:

- 2 cups breadcrumbs
- 2 eggs, beaten
- Vegetable oil for frying

Instructions:

1. In a medium saucepan, heat the olive oil over medium heat. Add the chopped onion and cook until softened, about 5 minutes. Add the minced garlic and cook for an additional 1-2 minutes, until fragrant.
2. Stir in the diced red bell pepper and tomato, and cook for another 5 minutes, until the vegetables are softened.
3. Add the paella rice to the saucepan and toast it for 1-2 minutes, stirring constantly.
4. Pour in the chicken or seafood broth and add the saffron threads (if using), smoked paprika, turmeric, salt, and pepper. Stir well to combine.
5. Bring the mixture to a simmer, then reduce the heat to low and cover the saucepan with a lid. Cook for 15-20 minutes, or until the rice is tender and has absorbed the liquid.
6. Once the rice is cooked, stir in the thawed peas and chopped fresh parsley. Remove the paella rice from the heat and let it cool slightly.
7. In a large mixing bowl, combine the cooked and chopped mixed seafood with chopped fresh parsley. Season with salt and pepper to taste.
8. Take small portions of the cooled paella rice mixture and flatten them in the palm of your hand. Place a spoonful of the seafood filling in the center of each flattened portion of rice.
9. Fold the rice around the seafood filling to enclose it completely, shaping it into a ball. Repeat with the remaining rice and seafood filling to make all the paella balls.
10. Set up a breading station with three shallow dishes: one with breadcrumbs, one with beaten eggs, and one empty.
11. Dip each paella ball first into the beaten eggs, then into the breadcrumbs, coating them evenly.
12. Heat vegetable oil in a deep fryer or large skillet to 350°F (175°C).
13. Fry the breaded paella balls in the hot oil, a few at a time, until they are golden brown and crispy, about 2-3 minutes per batch.
14. Remove the fried paella balls from the oil and drain them on paper towels to remove excess oil.
15. Serve the seafood paella balls hot, garnished with additional chopped fresh parsley if desired.
16. Enjoy these delicious seafood paella balls as a flavorful appetizer or snack!

These seafood paella balls are sure to be a hit with seafood lovers, combining the flavors of paella with the convenience of bite-sized, crispy balls. Enjoy!

Corn Chips with Guacamole and Salsa

Ingredients:

For the guacamole:

- 2 ripe avocados
- 1 small red onion, finely diced
- 1-2 cloves garlic, minced
- 1 small tomato, diced
- Juice of 1 lime
- 2 tablespoons chopped fresh cilantro
- Salt and pepper to taste

For the salsa:

- 2 medium tomatoes, diced
- 1/2 small red onion, finely diced
- 1/4 cup chopped fresh cilantro
- Juice of 1 lime
- 1 jalapeño pepper, seeded and finely diced (optional for heat)
- Salt and pepper to taste

For serving:

- Corn chips (tortilla chips)

Instructions:

1. To make the guacamole, cut the avocados in half and remove the pits. Scoop the flesh into a bowl and mash it with a fork until smooth or chunky, depending on your preference.
2. Add the finely diced red onion, minced garlic, diced tomato, lime juice, chopped cilantro, salt, and pepper to the mashed avocado. Stir until well combined.
3. Taste the guacamole and adjust the seasoning if needed. Add more salt, pepper, or lime juice to taste. Cover the guacamole with plastic wrap, pressing it directly onto the surface to prevent browning, and refrigerate until ready to serve.

4. To make the salsa, combine the diced tomatoes, finely diced red onion, chopped cilantro, lime juice, and diced jalapeño pepper (if using) in a bowl. Season with salt and pepper to taste and stir until well combined.
5. Taste the salsa and adjust the seasoning if needed. Add more salt, pepper, or lime juice to taste. Cover the salsa and refrigerate until ready to serve.
6. When ready to serve, arrange the corn chips on a serving platter or in a bowl.
7. Place the guacamole and salsa in separate bowls and serve alongside the corn chips.
8. Enjoy the corn chips with guacamole and salsa as a tasty appetizer or snack!

Feel free to customize the guacamole and salsa to your taste preferences by adding additional ingredients such as diced jalapeños, chopped bell peppers, or minced garlic. Serve them with your favorite corn chips for a delicious and satisfying snack that's sure to be a hit with friends and family.

Tandoori Chicken Wings

Ingredients:

For the marinade:

- 2 lbs (about 900g) chicken wings, split at the joints and tips removed
- 1 cup plain yogurt
- 3 tablespoons tandoori masala spice blend
- 2 tablespoons lemon juice
- 2 cloves garlic, minced
- 1 tablespoon grated ginger
- 1 teaspoon ground cumin
- 1 teaspoon ground coriander
- 1 teaspoon smoked paprika
- 1/2 teaspoon turmeric
- 1/2 teaspoon cayenne pepper (adjust to taste for spice level)
- Salt to taste

For serving:

- Fresh lemon wedges
- Chopped cilantro leaves (optional)
- Mint yogurt sauce or raita (optional)

Instructions:

1. In a large bowl, whisk together the plain yogurt, tandoori masala spice blend, lemon juice, minced garlic, grated ginger, ground cumin, ground coriander, smoked paprika, turmeric, cayenne pepper, and salt to taste until well combined.
2. Add the chicken wings to the marinade, making sure they are evenly coated. Cover the bowl with plastic wrap and refrigerate for at least 2 hours, or overnight for best results, to allow the flavors to meld and the chicken to marinate.
3. Preheat your grill to medium-high heat or preheat your oven to 400°F (200°C). If using a grill, lightly oil the grate to prevent sticking.

4. Remove the marinated chicken wings from the refrigerator and let them come to room temperature while the grill or oven is heating up.
5. If using a grill, place the chicken wings on the preheated grill and cook for 20-25 minutes, turning occasionally, until they are cooked through and have charred grill marks on all sides.
6. If using an oven, arrange the chicken wings on a baking sheet lined with aluminum foil or parchment paper. Bake in the preheated oven for 25-30 minutes, turning halfway through, until they are cooked through and golden brown.
7. Once the chicken wings are cooked, remove them from the grill or oven and transfer them to a serving platter.
8. Serve the tandoori chicken wings hot, garnished with fresh lemon wedges and chopped cilantro leaves if desired. Serve mint yogurt sauce or raita on the side for dipping.
9. Enjoy these flavorful tandoori chicken wings as a delicious appetizer or main dish!

These tandoori chicken wings are sure to be a hit at your next gathering with their bold flavors and juicy, tender meat. Adjust the level of cayenne pepper to suit your spice preference, and feel free to customize the marinade with additional spices or herbs for your own twist on this classic Indian dish.

Feta and Olive Stuffed Peppers

Ingredients:

- 6 large bell peppers, any color
- 4 oz (115g) feta cheese, crumbled
- 1/4 cup Kalamata olives, pitted and chopped
- 1/4 cup sun-dried tomatoes, chopped
- 2 tablespoons chopped fresh parsley
- 1 tablespoon chopped fresh basil
- 2 cloves garlic, minced
- 2 tablespoons olive oil
- Salt and pepper to taste
- Optional: additional herbs or spices to taste, such as oregano or red pepper flakes

Instructions:

1. Preheat your oven to 375°F (190°C). Lightly grease a baking dish large enough to hold the peppers upright.
2. Cut the tops off the bell peppers and remove the seeds and membranes from the insides. Rinse the peppers under cold water and pat them dry with paper towels.
3. In a mixing bowl, combine the crumbled feta cheese, chopped Kalamata olives, chopped sun-dried tomatoes, chopped fresh parsley, chopped fresh basil, minced garlic, olive oil, and any optional herbs or spices. Stir well to combine.
4. Season the feta and olive mixture with salt and pepper to taste.
5. Stuff each bell pepper with the feta and olive mixture, pressing it down gently to fill the peppers completely.
6. Place the stuffed peppers upright in the prepared baking dish.
7. Cover the baking dish with aluminum foil and bake in the preheated oven for 25-30 minutes, or until the peppers are tender and the filling is heated through.
8. Remove the foil from the baking dish and bake for an additional 5-10 minutes, or until the tops of the peppers are lightly golden brown.
9. Remove the stuffed peppers from the oven and let them cool slightly before serving.
10. Serve the feta and olive stuffed peppers warm as a delicious appetizer or side dish.

These feta and olive stuffed peppers are flavorful and satisfying, with the tangy saltiness of the feta cheese complementing the briny richness of the olives and the sweetness of the peppers. Enjoy them as a tasty addition to your next meal!

Chicken Liver Pate on Toast Points

Ingredients:

For the chicken liver pâté:

- 1 lb (450g) chicken livers, trimmed
- 1 onion, finely chopped
- 2 cloves garlic, minced
- 4 tablespoons unsalted butter
- 2 tablespoons brandy or cognac (optional)
- 1 teaspoon fresh thyme leaves (or 1/2 teaspoon dried thyme)
- 1/4 teaspoon ground nutmeg
- Salt and pepper to taste
- 1/2 cup heavy cream

For the toast points:

- Sliced French baguette or bread of your choice
- Olive oil or melted butter for brushing

Instructions:

1. In a large skillet, melt 2 tablespoons of butter over medium heat. Add the finely chopped onion and minced garlic, and cook until softened and translucent, about 3-4 minutes.
2. Add the chicken livers to the skillet and cook until browned on the outside but still slightly pink on the inside, about 2-3 minutes per side.
3. Remove the skillet from the heat and let the mixture cool slightly.
4. Transfer the cooked chicken livers, onions, and garlic to a food processor. Add the remaining 2 tablespoons of butter, brandy or cognac (if using), fresh thyme leaves, ground nutmeg, salt, and pepper.
5. Pulse the mixture in the food processor until smooth and creamy, scraping down the sides of the bowl as needed.

6. With the food processor running, slowly pour in the heavy cream and continue to process until the pâté is smooth and creamy. Taste and adjust the seasoning if needed.
7. Transfer the chicken liver pâté to a serving dish or individual ramekins, cover, and refrigerate for at least 2 hours to allow the flavors to meld and the pâté to set.
8. While the pâté is chilling, preheat your oven to 375°F (190°C). Place the sliced baguette or bread on a baking sheet in a single layer.
9. Brush the bread slices lightly with olive oil or melted butter.
10. Bake the bread slices in the preheated oven for 8-10 minutes, or until they are golden brown and crisp.
11. Remove the toast points from the oven and let them cool slightly.
12. To serve, spread the chilled chicken liver pâté onto the toast points and arrange them on a serving platter.
13. Garnish the chicken liver pâté with fresh herbs, such as parsley or thyme, if desired.
14. Serve the chicken liver pâté on toast points as a delicious appetizer or starter.

Enjoy the rich and creamy flavor of the chicken liver pâté paired with the crispy texture of the toast points. It's sure to be a hit at your next gathering or dinner party!

Aussie BBQ Shrimp

Ingredients:

- 1 lb (450g) large shrimp, peeled and deveined, tails left on
- 2 tablespoons olive oil
- 2 cloves garlic, minced
- 1 tablespoon lemon juice
- 1 teaspoon paprika
- 1/2 teaspoon chili powder (optional, for a spicy kick)
- Salt and pepper to taste
- Lemon wedges, for serving
- Chopped fresh parsley, for garnish (optional)

Instructions:

1. In a large bowl, combine the olive oil, minced garlic, lemon juice, paprika, chili powder (if using), salt, and pepper. Stir well to combine.
2. Add the peeled and deveined shrimp to the bowl, tossing to coat them evenly in the marinade. Cover the bowl and refrigerate for at least 30 minutes to allow the flavors to meld.
3. Preheat your grill to medium-high heat. If using wooden skewers, soak them in water for at least 30 minutes to prevent them from burning.
4. Thread the marinated shrimp onto skewers, leaving a little space between each shrimp.
5. Once the grill is hot, place the shrimp skewers directly onto the grill grates. Cook for 2-3 minutes per side, or until the shrimp are opaque and pink, with grill marks on both sides.
6. Remove the shrimp skewers from the grill and transfer them to a serving platter.
7. Garnish the Aussie BBQ shrimp with chopped fresh parsley, if desired, and serve immediately with lemon wedges on the side for squeezing over the shrimp.
8. Enjoy the Aussie BBQ shrimp hot off the grill as a delicious appetizer or main dish.

These Aussie BBQ shrimp are sure to be a hit at your next barbecue with their bold flavors and succulent texture. Serve them with your favorite sides and enjoy the taste of summer!

Veggie and Cheese Mini Quiches

Ingredients:

- 1 sheet of store-bought puff pastry, thawed
- 1 tablespoon olive oil
- 1/2 cup diced bell peppers (any color)
- 1/2 cup diced onions
- 1/2 cup diced mushrooms
- 1/2 cup chopped spinach or kale
- 1/2 cup shredded cheese (cheddar, mozzarella, or your favorite)
- 4 large eggs
- 1/2 cup milk or cream
- Salt and pepper to taste
- Optional: chopped fresh herbs such as parsley or chives

Instructions:

1. Preheat your oven to 375°F (190°C). Lightly grease a mini muffin tin with cooking spray or butter.
2. Roll out the thawed puff pastry sheet on a lightly floured surface. Using a round cookie cutter or a glass, cut out circles of dough slightly larger than the muffin tin cavities. Press each circle of dough into the cavities to form the crusts for the mini quiches. Prick the bottoms of the pastry crusts with a fork to prevent them from puffing up too much during baking.
3. In a skillet, heat the olive oil over medium heat. Add the diced bell peppers, onions, and mushrooms, and sauté until they are softened, about 5-7 minutes. Add the chopped spinach or kale and cook for an additional 2-3 minutes, until wilted. Remove from heat and let the mixture cool slightly.
4. In a mixing bowl, whisk together the eggs, milk or cream, salt, and pepper until well combined.
5. Stir the cooled vegetable mixture and shredded cheese into the egg mixture until evenly distributed.
6. Spoon the egg and vegetable mixture into each pastry crust, filling them almost to the top.
7. Bake the mini quiches in the preheated oven for 15-20 minutes, or until the pastry is golden brown and the filling is set.

8. Remove the mini quiches from the oven and let them cool slightly in the muffin tin before carefully removing them.
9. Serve the veggie and cheese mini quiches warm or at room temperature, garnished with chopped fresh herbs if desired.

These veggie and cheese mini quiches are versatile and can be customized with your favorite vegetables and cheese combinations. They're great for brunch, parties, or even as a quick and easy meal prep option. Enjoy!

Stuffed Dates with Prosciutto and Goat Cheese

Ingredients:

- 12 large Medjool dates, pitted
- 4 oz (115g) soft goat cheese
- 6 slices prosciutto, halved lengthwise
- Freshly ground black pepper, to taste
- Optional: balsamic glaze or honey for drizzling

Instructions:

1. Preheat your oven to 375°F (190°C). Line a baking sheet with parchment paper or aluminum foil.
2. Make a small lengthwise slit in each date and gently remove the pit, being careful not to tear the date completely in half.
3. Fill each pitted date with a small spoonful of goat cheese, using your fingers or the back of a spoon to press the cheese into the date.
4. Wrap each stuffed date with a half slice of prosciutto, ensuring that the date is completely covered.
5. Place the stuffed dates seam-side down on the prepared baking sheet. Sprinkle freshly ground black pepper over the top of each date, if desired.
6. Bake the stuffed dates in the preheated oven for 10-12 minutes, or until the prosciutto is crispy and the goat cheese is slightly melted.
7. Remove the stuffed dates from the oven and let them cool slightly before serving.
8. Optional: Drizzle the stuffed dates with balsamic glaze or honey for a touch of sweetness and extra flavor.
9. Serve the stuffed dates with prosciutto and goat cheese warm or at room temperature as a delicious appetizer or snack.

These stuffed dates with prosciutto and goat cheese are sure to impress your guests with their combination of sweet, salty, and creamy flavors. They're perfect for entertaining or as a luxurious treat for yourself. Enjoy!

Grilled Lamb Cutlets with Mint Sauce

Ingredients:

For the lamb cutlets:

- 8 lamb cutlets
- 2 tablespoons olive oil
- 2 cloves garlic, minced
- 1 tablespoon fresh rosemary, chopped
- Salt and pepper to taste

For the mint sauce:

- 1/2 cup fresh mint leaves, finely chopped
- 2 tablespoons white wine vinegar
- 1 tablespoon sugar
- 2 tablespoons boiling water

Instructions:

1. Preheat your grill to medium-high heat.
2. In a small bowl, combine the olive oil, minced garlic, chopped rosemary, salt, and pepper. Mix well to combine.
3. Rub the seasoned olive oil mixture all over the lamb cutlets, coating them evenly.
4. Place the lamb cutlets on the preheated grill and cook for 3-4 minutes per side, or until they are cooked to your desired level of doneness. For medium-rare, the internal temperature should reach 145°F (63°C).
5. While the lamb cutlets are cooking, prepare the mint sauce. In a heatproof bowl, combine the finely chopped mint leaves, white wine vinegar, and sugar.
6. Pour the boiling water over the mint mixture and stir until the sugar is dissolved.
7. Let the mint sauce sit for a few minutes to allow the flavors to meld together.
8. Once the lamb cutlets are cooked, remove them from the grill and let them rest for a few minutes before serving.
9. Serve the grilled lamb cutlets hot, accompanied by the mint sauce on the side.

10. Enjoy the delicious combination of tender grilled lamb and refreshing mint sauce!

Grilled lamb cutlets with mint sauce are best served with your favorite sides, such as roasted vegetables, couscous, or a fresh salad. They're sure to impress your family and friends with their flavor and elegance. Enjoy!

www.ingramcontent.com/pod-product-compliance
Lightning Source LLC
LaVergne TN
LVHW061943070526
838199LV00060B/3942